The Body

Muscles

Veronica Ross

Chrysalis Education

Distributed in the United States by
Smart Apple Media
2140 Howard Drive West
North Mankato, Minnesota 56003

ISBN 1-59389-166-0

Library of Congress control number: 2004043807

Editorial manager: Joyce Bentley
Editors: Rosalind Beckman, Joe Fullman
Illustrator: Chris Forsey
Designer: Wladek Szechter
Picture researcher: Jenny Barlow

Printed in China

10 9 8 7 6 5 4 3 2 1

Words in **bold** can be found in Words to remember on page 30.

The pictures used in this book do not show the actual people named the text.

Picture credits
Angela Hampton/Family Life Picture Library: 10, 12, 13, 14, 17.
Chrysalis Images/Ray Moller: 7, 18, 20.
Corbis: LWA-Dann Tardif Front Cover (Main), 4, 5; Norbert Schaefer FC (Inset) , 1, 6; Jose Luis
Pelaez, Inc. FC (Inset), 9T; Larry Williams FC (Inset), 26; Gerhard Steiner FC (Inset), 24; Jim
Erickson 15; Franco Vogt 16; Darwin Wiggett 19; Strauss/Curtis 27.
Digital Vision: 9B.
Getty Images: Nick Clements 23.
ImageState: 21.
Stockbyte: 25.
Illustrations: Chris Forsey 8, 11, 22, 28, 29, back cover (inset).

Contents

Look at me!

I can jump. I can dance. I can **blink** and smile. **Muscles** all over my body help me to move and do all the things I want to do.

You use your muscles every time you move. Without them you could not run, walk, or jump.

Strong muscles
in your legs help
you to hop when
you play hopscotch.

Where are my muscles?

There are **muscles** all over your body. You have muscles in your face, head, tongue, neck, shoulders, chest, stomach, bottom, legs, arms, and hands. There are more muscles in your body than **bones**.

Stick out your tongue and wiggle it around. Your tongue is one of the most powerful muscles in your body.

You have more than 670 muscles in your body.

Do you **shrug** your shoulders if you don't know the answer to a question? The muscles in your shoulders help you do this.

What are muscles?

Muscles are the tough, stretchy parts in your body that help you to move. They come in different shapes and sizes, because they do different jobs.

This drawing shows the long muscles in your legs.

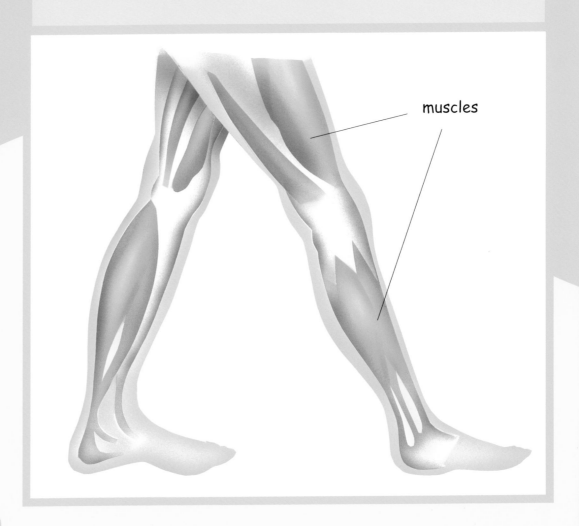

muscles

Some of the biggest muscles are in your back. These muscles help you bend and lift a heavy pile of books.

Small muscles around your eyes let you look up and down, and from side to side.

How do muscles work?

Many muscles work in pairs. They pull on the bones that form your **skeleton** and make them move.

You can see your muscles pushing up under your skin, when you bend your arm and make a fist.

All your muscles are **controlled** by your **brain**. It sends out messages to tell the muscles what to do.

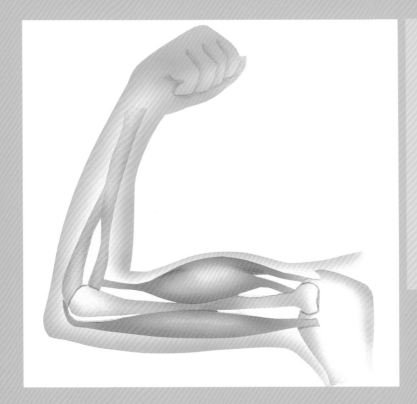

When you bend your arm, the muscle at the top of your arm gets thicker and shorter. It pulls on the bone in the front of your arm, to pull your arm up.

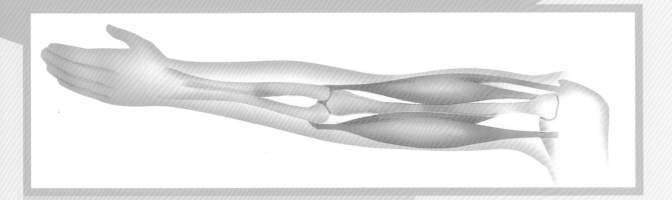

The muscle at the back of your arm pulls your arm down again.

Stomach muscles

The food that you swallow passes down a tube into your stomach. Strong muscles in your stomach walls help to turn the food around and squeeze it until it is soft and mushy.

Your stomach muscles help you to bend forward.

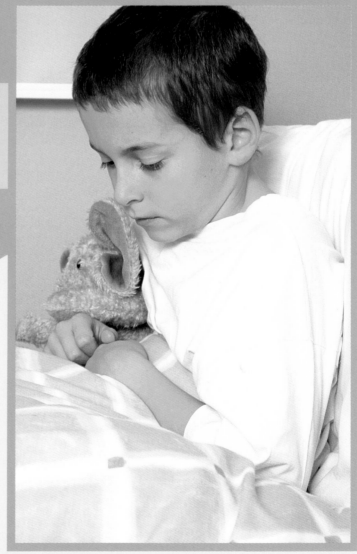

Your stomach muscles help you to bend over and touch your toes, and twist around.

When you throw up, the stomach muscles push the food back out of your stomach, up your throat, and out of your mouth. Yuk!

Arms and hands

Large, strong muscles in your arms give you strength to pick up things.

When you play the piano, your **brain** sends messages to your hand and wrist muscles to help them move your hands quickly across the keys.

Small muscles in your hands and wrists help you to make **delicate** movements, such as holding a pencil and writing a letter.

Hands and wrists move in lots of ways. You can grip a book and gently turn the pages.

Leg work

The muscles in your legs need to be strong, because they help to carry the weight of your body when you stand up and when you walk around.

Your leg muscles give you the power to jump high in the air.

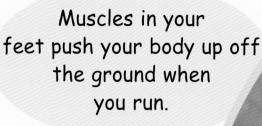

Muscles in your feet push your body up off the ground when you run.

Your muscles are very heavy. They make up half your body's weight.

Funny faces

There are lots of tiny muscles in your face. You use these muscles when you smile, **frown**, shout, and cry, and when you make silly faces.

When you are surprised, muscles open your mouth wide and raise your eyebrows.

When you smile, you use about 20 muscles, but when you frown, you use about 40 muscles. So it's easier to smile!

Look in a mirror and see how many different funny faces you can make.

On your bottom

Two big, rounded muscles cover the bony part of your bottom. When you sit down, the muscles make a soft, squashy cushion.

Sitting on the bony part of your bottom would be painful. Your bottom muscles pad the bone and make sitting down much more comfortable.

When you stand up, the muscles tighten
to pull your bottom upward and forward.

The muscles
in your bottom also
help to keep your
back straight.

Heartbeat

Your **heart** is a special type of muscle. It pumps **blood** around your body and **beats** all day and all night.

heart

Your heart is inside your chest.

The blood supplies your body with the **oxygen** it needs to make **energy**. Your heart works very hard, so it is a very strong muscle.

You can feel your heart beating if you have been running.

Feeding your muscles

Your muscles do a great job, but to keep them working properly, you need to take care of them. A good way to do this is to eat healthy food.

A breakfast of cereal, fruit, and a glass of milk is a good way to start the day.

Foods such as fruit and vegetables, beans, fish, and chicken will keep your muscles in good working order.

Body-building foods such as milk, cheese, nuts, and cereals are good for building muscles.

Exercise

Exercise is the best way to look after your muscles. It keeps them strong and **supple**.

Swimming makes the muscles in your legs and arms stronger.

Dancing, gymnastics, or just playing chase in the park are really good ways to exercise, and to keep fit and healthy.

Before you exercise, do some stretching and bending to warm up. If your muscles are warm, they will work better.

Sometimes muscles **tear**. This can happen if you fall or exercise too hard. Resting will help the muscle heal.

Muscles at work

Now that you know where some of your muscles are, try these exercises and see if you can feel the muscles working.

Bend your leg as if you were about to kick a ball. Can you feel the muscles at the back of your leg tighten? Now kick the ball and feel the muscles at the back of your leg **relax**.

Try moving
your head up and down
to feel the muscles
in your neck.

beat To pump. When your heart beats, it pumps blood around your body.

blink To close your eyes for a second.

bones The hard, tough parts inside your body that make up your skeleton.

blood The red liquid full of oxygen that is pumped around your body by your heart.

brain The soft part inside your head that controls everything you think and do.

control To be in charge of things that happen.

delicate Something that is very precious and needs special care. Delicate movements are careful and gentle.

energy The power you need to be able to do all the things you want to do.

frown To look worried or angry.

heart The muscle that pumps blood around your body.

muscles The soft, stretchy parts inside your body that make you move.

oxygen A gas found in the air that you need in order to breathe.

relax To make your muscles looser.

shrug To raise your shoulders. You might shrug if you don't know the answer to a question.

skeleton All the bones in your body.

stomach A large muscle in your body where food is stored before it is broken down to be digested by your body.

supple Moving and bending easily.

tear To rip and come apart.

Index